S0-BNJ-290

CHASING THE RAVEN

CHASING THE RAVEN

CHRISTOPHER SOUTHGATE

Shoestring Press

All rights reserved. No part of this work covered by the copyright herein may be reproduced or used in any means – graphic, electronic, or mechanical, including copying, recording, taping, or information storage and retrieval systems – without written permission of the publisher.

Printed by imprintdigital
Upton Pyne, Exeter
www.imprintdigital.com

Typesetting and cover design by narrator
www.narrator.me.uk
info@narrator.me.uk
033 022 300 39

Published by Shoestring Press
19 Devonshire Avenue, Beeston, Nottingham, NG9 1BS
(0115) 925 1827
www.shoestringpress.co.uk

First published 2016
© Copyright: Christopher Southgate

The moral right of the author has been asserted.

Front cover photograph by Frankie Fraser
Back cover photograph by Stuart Webb

ISBN 978-1-910323-61-8

ACKNOWLEDGEMENTS

'Return to Ground Zero, 2012' was previously published in the journal *Spiritus*.

I thank all those poets who have offered critical encouragement in the making of these poems, especially colleagues at the Company of Poets, also Andy Brown, Chris Considine, Hilary Menos, Julie-Ann Rowell, Richard Skinner, Dana Littlepage Smith, and Anthony Wilson.

As ever I thank my editor John Lucas for his continuing support and affirmation.

Lastly I thank with my whole heart my wife Sandy, whose friendship and love have made all these explorations possible.

CONTENTS

I

WHEN

I. When everything seemed possible

There's a stain on my old cagoule
from a pool of boat-oil in the bottom of the dinghy
that took us across Loch Broom.

It is a stain from – not a simpler time –
but a time of less history, less regret.
Sun setting into the Atlantic
casting copper colours onto the hills,
possibilities at the flood.

That I would boldly encounter
        the lover I longed for.
That I would make a career, make a mark,
        in some esoteric field.
That I would discover
        how to be with people
beyond shyness.

The stain fades with age and sweat.
Life silts up with missed chances
        and too much unkindness.
If one had only known then
        by the loch-shore
how to place pebbles
        on a woman's naked back
how to delight in haiku
        without counting the syllables
how to act under pressure
        how to speak without acting.

But then one wouldn't have been
the wide-eyed callow zestful youth
staring into the sun-blazed ocean, the coppered hills
and thinking everything possible.

3

II. Just about as good as it gets

Caffè Reggio, Greenwich Village, autumn

I snaffle
    the one table under the light.
I successfully fight off
    the lure of my first ever zabaglione.
I order
    their time-honoured cappuccino.
I plan
    a poetry reading for a good friend
and think about
    how the late afternoon light in Manhattan
    disappears from ground level
    but echoes around high buildings
    singing off glass
    turning brick to vermilion
    lifting the heart.

I walk back
    through the Square, thinking of moves at chess.
A Japanese student
    is teaching his girlfriend
    to shoot freethrows in the dark
A gingko in a courtyard
    has leaves in yellow helices,
    stitched cascades of grace.
In a borrowed apartment,
    Number Two Fifth Avenue, sheets of silk,
    my best friend, waiting.

III. The last time things made any sense

I can identify it exactly.
It was during the Arab Spring.
From separate adventures
we were walking back to our bus-stop in Florence
and our eyes met by the Innocenti.
Where we were, where we were going,
framed in precise arches of lucent stone.
Fierce sea-beasts served as fountains.

The fight for freedom has reached a new phase
called civil war. Our country tries to decide
who to aid, who to bomb.
Loved colleagues leave, and bullies thrive.
Young friends test positive for life-threateners.
We do not now walk in step
                              even into carnival.
The village rooks mock my studies of glory.

I can be forgiven
for living in that kiss of the eyes
across a Florentine square.
An oasis of coinciding, exactly.
I can be forgiven.

STORIES

The expert from Leiden, beautiful
English, singing Dutch intonation,
Dissects history. Eighth-century Turkmenistan
Is not as we had always thought.
As for the story that Chinese prisoners
Gave paper-making to the Arab world
Well – she laughs, *cantabile* –
                    I love that story, but..

I love the story that the Lord God planted a garden
Eastward in Eden, where a couple lived in innocence.
But there never was a talking snake
Or a benign rapport with birds and beasts.
In the cool of the day
They trapped and hunted, laughed and fought
And made children.
                    God watched, longingly.

I love the story that my mother's family
Were Huguenot refugees, and silversmiths,
And kept a two-handled cup, worn thin with age,
From the time of their exile. But
The cup is not hallmarked La Rochelle
And the silversmith was, prosaically,
The one son too many
                    Of a London solicitor.

I love the story that after our eyes met
Across that pot-hazed room
I never looked at another woman
You never hated my cool English stubbornness
We were always good-enough parents
And we never wasted the gifts
That we were given.
                    I love that story.

IN MEMORIAM FRED SANGER, BIOCHEMICAL SEQUENCER

I am sixteen. The University department
send a biochemist up to my school. He challenges us
to find a way to sequence a five-residue peptide.
To be, in miniature, Sanger wrestling with insulin.
I contribute a key suggestion. I am hooked,
into this one-dimensional world of meticulous decoding.

At twenty-four, finishing a PhD, I get to spend a fortnight
in the halls of the MRC Lab. Here they are, wandering down the corridors,
quizzing me by the scintillation counter, lending me equipment,
the high-priests of my world – Sanger, Fersht, Klug, Perutz.
It is like.. It is like knocking up with Nadal, using an old racket of Federer's.
It is like workshopping poems with Ted Hughes,
the pencil judiciously sharpened by Larkin.
I want the fortnight to last forever.

And yet my favourite moments are on the drive home every night
(I finish, reluctantly, around eleven, am back at eight).
I take the short-cut through Grantchester, cross the river,
moonlight echoing through the deep-thinking willow trees.
Rupert Brooke consults the clock, goes off to war. I assemble
enough scraps of data for my first ever paper.
I cannot quite credit that this time of scintillations, this moon,
are joined up with my other life, my other longings.

At fifty-four, I hear a sociologist analysing Sanger's lab diaries.
He was held back, I learn, by being trapped in the language
of codes and master-molecules. His mind was hemmed in by the
                                                        Cold War.
Poor old Fred. Trapped and hemmed,
he managed only two Nobel Prizes.
inspired only thousands of young researchers.

He has died at ninety-five. Refused a knighthood. Accepted an OM.
Covered in glory, of the quiet scientific kind.
If only he had known some sociology.

SHE WAS IN OUR YEAR

For MCAG

We stare into a keen wind
under a low sun.
The eulogy gives us structure
sinews of an academic life
lived with passion
facing up to truths.
We face a fact
older than convention.
It blows full in our faces
over the untended wicker coffin
nested with flowers.
If it blows into us
it will erode hope
separate sinews.
So we use ancient words –
Shakespeare, Qoheleth –
practised channellers
taking the wind
on safe paths through souls.
We step forward
scatter earth from a safe distance
and say framing words
from ground that is not anger,
or anguish.
We give those most affected
the space we need.
When we are unobserved
we clean the earth
from under fingernails
and forge on
under a shortened light.

CONSTANCY

"When the young duke spoke so kindly to me there was no need
to feel like weeping, that was foolish. I must keep my head up
and smile."
– from Philippa Gregory's novel *The Constant Princess*

Such is my worry and sadness
That I take to reading historical novels.
The princess responds to the young duke's
Kindness. Her tears are safe centuries away.
They help me keep my head up and smile.

Such is my mind's stalled turmoil
That even a day's delay in one of your clinics
Spins me into chaos. I phone and phone
'Choose and Book', my voice breaking.
But in person I keep my head up, and smile.

Such is the brightness of this spurious sunlight
That it does not take a duke's kindness
To make my eyes water. But provided
I am always careful, and not caught out,
I can keep my head up and smile.

It would only take a careful word,
Or a pastoral arm around my shoulder
While I am apart from you, to dissolve
My regime. But day after cautious day, invisible,
I keep my head up and smile.

It would only take one adverse test
For ferritin, or alkaline phosphatase,
Or some new marker I have never even heard of,
To ransack what is left of my resolve.
I keep my head up, and smile.

What breaks me and makes me
Is your voice on the phone, which plays
The same tune on my spirit as when we first loved.
It turns my head. It tears up my plans.
Inside I smile, and cry and cry and cry.

BLOOD AND INCUBATORS

Our lives are lived in waiting-rooms
from which you are called
to supply yet more blood
for yet more tests.
We try to construct meaning
in a time of waiting.
We stare at numbers as they traverse
the consultant's screens. We crumple
in the crumple-zone of the hospital chapel
under an unseeing crucifix.

In a foreign city
I go for an appointment
in what is called an incubator.
I think of babies
but there are none here
only sharp glass cubicles
and sharp young people saving the world.
A woman tells me
                quite suddenly in the elevator
that my attitude is not positive enough.

Your blood is used to incubate whatever.
The consultant tells us
some markers are weakly positive
for what might
or might not be treatable.
I practise my positives. I pray to know
how to treat whatever the news is
of the body I love.

The world goes on
being saved,
by blood and incubators.

MINDING THE GAP

Munich, 2015

I am escorted on the U-bahn
by my urban-savvy goddaughter
who knows exactly where on the platform
will save seconds at the Hauptbahnhof. We buy
salami and designer water
and locate the platform for Vienna.
I have my window-seat reservation,
a huge hug goodbye
and my e-ticket to fly home Monday.

String-bags. Syrian sandals
worn to the rim.
                At every border
stretching queues and twisted wire.
Piling onto a suddenly-arriving train
clutching children.
                They reach destinations
occasionally to applause and soup. More often
to rejection, rough quotas at best.

There is a gap at the Hauptbahnhof
a light-second wide.
Between us the same night
thickens and falls.

Note: *a light-second – the distance travelled by light in a second,*
approximately 186,000 miles.

RUSSELL SQUARE – SUMMER

I have started to study men older than myself,
investigating what life might hold,
how long vigour remains in the stride.

I am interrupted by designer sunglasses
walking fast, discoursing earnestly with an unknown
stranger, hands free, heart intent,

and by the protocols of new lovers
lying down on the grass. How much skin
will be shown? Who will hold the ice-cream?

The plane trees, weary of new lovers,
preferring this slanting sunlight to ice-cream,
measure their way towards evening.

They have started to study trees older than themselves
wondering how long vigour
remains in the stride.

But they, and lovers old and new,
and even the most earnest sunglasses
all stop when a small child squeals,
jumping with delight through the fountains.

I HEAR MY FATHER

I hear my father
more and more these days,
at shop counters,
in clinics, and the offices
of solicitors.
I see him give that
slightly staring, slightly apprehensive
impression, hear him trying as ever
to convey all the right signals.

That he *can* afford
whatever it is
indeed that he could afford the best there is
though today he does not choose to.
(Next time, perhaps, if they are courteous
and good to him.)
Furthermore that he *is* someone
in other spheres
and more than capable
of filing a complaint
of the most devastating kind
if he is ever crossed.
And that he is disposed to be nice
on this occasion, but he *is*
in something of a hurry.

I hear myself say, silently,
Back off. Just be ordinary.
Then, pleadingly,
Don't flirt.
Thirty years too late for that
and so embarrassing.
And then, louder, shouting without sound,
For God's sake don't overdo the power thing,
and try not to be so anxious.

My father never listened.
His face, a lion
and a slightly lost puppy,
stares back at me
from the plain mirror
they have so inconsiderately placed
behind the head of whoever it is
I am seeking to impress.

IN THE ZONE

In my dream they come to tell me
a friend of mine did not make it.
He took his own life after a long struggle
with all the usual pills, and heartbreak.
The funeral will be delayed
while the family takes stock.
A human life has weight, needs space to lose.

It was a strange dream to have.
This friend of mine was killed in a car crash
when we were both eighteen.
He was brilliant, bold, reckless
lacking all doubt in the world.
In forty years I have not wondered once
about the man he might have become.

I drive to work in the dark.
Later, I queue for the car-park
to queue for outpatients, to get the injections
that will keep me productive.
I am summoned to meetings at which
someone is deputed to tell me
what will be required, over and above.

Hemmed in, the mind roams wild –
tries out death, re-enacts it,
works out its ironies
in a far-off zone.

THE WATER-MARK

Thinking, in springtime, of all your pain
mocks my every thought of love,
reminds me how chatter about my book
and planned sabbatical in Italy
used up your scarce time, freely given,
was like ignoring falling water.

An intricately laid-out water
garden, framed by concrete blocks. Pain
constrained everything, became a given,
droned across attempts at talk of love.
We were as shy as long ago in Italy
when all of culture seemed an open book.

On every birthday I had sent you the book
I most admired, and felt the cool water
of your appreciation. Diaries of Italy,
allusive sonnets. Desperate at your pain
I sent more and more tokens of unspoken love –
withholding what I should have given.

What I ought at least to have offered, if not given,
but was too afraid, had hidden it in a book
of poems, long since out of print. Love
is not so easily remaindered. Springs of water
do not just disappear. But pain
can poison them, can blur memories of Italy.

I did not see your tears at talk of Italy.
I had not heard the hints you'd given.
I could not taste the acrid taste of pain,
feel the agony in arms too weak to hold a book.
The wine of your life was turned to water,
lost its savour. You lost belief in love.

Those who had guessed at our love
hated my decision to spend that spring in Italy.
They saw it as escape, putting clear water
between myself and hurt. But you had given
leave. Your last smile, a coded book,
foretold the overdose, left me the pain.

To dream of love, freely given
and received, then book a flight to Italy
was to water-mark all sunlight with memories of pain.

TRUTHS AT THE AIRPORT

She tells me in the departure lounge
that it's not about memory
that every moment is to be received
and lived in.

Lived from, I correct her
in my head. I do not want
to take issue with this young and holy
earnestness.

I want to receive it
while it lasts, while we
and our partners sit in this synthetic lounge
and drink and laugh together.

I promise to do better
about the present moment.
We are interrupted by a customer survey
of overall satisfaction

for which we each receive a free pen.
Neuroscientists tell us it lasts three seconds
(the present moment, that is,
not overall satisfaction).

The length of an average line of poetry.

I retain from that day the free pen,
and the piquant memory of being lectured, lovingly,
by an atheist, on my spiritual unsoundness.
A moment to live from.

MERRIPIT HILL

A pianist from Norway.
He wraps his heavy accent
Round baffling English vowels.
He explains how he puzzles
Over the Goldberg Variations.
Every day they seem different,
Call for a different response,
A new emotional strategy.

And so with my memories.
Every day they seem different…
All these valleys I drive through
Are marked by past exhilarations
And mistakes, too many mistakes.
There were moments of possibility.
Misplaced shyness, mistimed boldness
Closed them off, consigned them to regret.

The keys are familiar, singing zest
Of prizes and early loves.
Bitterness of failure, and of so much loss.
Reaching mountain ridges
And looking down the deep plunge
Of the world. Gentle reassurance
Of first prayers, worship's exultation and emptiness.
Waking to my lover's many moods.

But they shift continually.
Colours sweep across them
And their balance changes.
All too often, delight is occluded.
Only very straight playing
Accurately re-performs gales of failure.
Only a detached tenderness
Keeps wistfulness in its proper place.

The high moor in winter, after rain.
Brown and sleet-grey slopes absorb it all.
Set your emotional strategies, they say.
We shall bury them. Every day
I puzzle over transience. But out here,
Wind high and scouring,
I come to feel a sort of freedom to celebrate
The gift of what was, improvisations on trust,

Release from the need to keep forgiving myself
For so many sacraments squandered.

BEFORE THE END

Ask me whether/what I have done is my life (William Stafford)
The facts about the world are not the end of the matter.
(Ludwig Wittgenstein)

Ask me facts about the world
From a time before I had done much.
I knew loads.

Ask me the end of the matter.
I can refer you to commentators
Giving every shade of opinion.

The facts about the world
Include data from my life –
All those I was seen to love.

The facts about the world
Include contracting possibilities.
What I have done is behind me.

The end of the matter
Is the moment just passed –
That graze of sun across a maple branch.

The end of the matter
Never comes while I still have
An ounce of longing in my heart.

Ask me, then, before the end,
My last prayer
And the whole surfeit of my dreams.

II

THREE RE-TELLINGS

I. Death at Troy

No kings came to weep over the body.
He was not liked – glory in its pure form
is not liked. Admired, emulated,
gossiped about, hated. Achilles
knew all these.
         The second spear the goddess
slipped into his hand
         slipped out of his hand.
Thetis' spell failed at the sky-god's whim.
Hector's sword entered at the groin, twisted,
emptied out guts and glory.

There was a subtle coup at the camp.
Odysseus, quiet as John Major,
assumed command. Agamemnon accepted exile
on Lesbos. With a good wind for Ithaca
the new chief obligingly dropped him off.
Hector, weary of dragging renown
through the dust, slept with the lovely Helen.
He was the only Trojan
         who had shown her kindness.
Something in her limpid eyes
         told him it was the time.

Paris shot him as he swam in the Scamander –
the armour of Achilles, bright as a hundred suns,
discarded on the bank.

II. Dante and Beatrice

I came to realise I would lose the loved face.
Neither of us wanted to ask forgiveness.
Neither of us had known such sadness in grace.

The chapel, kneeling at vespers, was the first place
We ever touched, first transient tenderness.
I came to realise I would lose the loved face.

We walked and walked, the city suddenly all menace,
All eyes and threats, sinister quietness.
Neither of us had known such sadness in grace.

The sex was awkward, angular, no trace
Of ecstasy, exchanging desperateness,
I came to realise I would lose the loved face.

Nothing in my memory will efface
That early touch, our only night, her nakedness.
Neither of us had known such sadness in grace.

We gave everything, gained nothing, each caress
More intense than the last. More hopeless.
I came to realise I had lost the loved face.
Neither of us had known such sadness in grace.

III. Prejudice ever after

Dear Jane
How I wish you would come to Pemberley!
Our society is very dismal here.
One should always trust one's first impressions.
He is just, alas, what we first saw –
All demands, and standards chosen by him
Highly selectively I may say.
My only refuge is this notebook and precious thoughts of you.

Dear Fitzwilliam
I fear it has been a hard year
In the odious state one calls matrimony.
She is always reading when I want to fuck
She is always writing when I want to talk.
She calls it, I believe, a novel
An inconceivably vulgar notion
In a lady of county standing.

I shall go abroad, I think,
And live in Venice with Brideshead
Or in Rome with Gilbert Osmond.
They seem to have clearer notions
                    About difficult wives.
Meanwhile, please come and hunt my new coverts.
Mellors has them in excellent order.

THREE COUNTERFACTUALS

I. Stauffenberg

On the phone Nina tells him
that where he has hidden her
is so quiet
she can hear the children breathing
as they sleep.

At the Wolf's Lair
the meeting is moved at the last moment
from the temporary shed back to the Führerbunker.
The walls are two metres thick. There are no windows.
The blast from the bomb kills everyone.

Job done, he assumes command in Berlin,
phones the Swedish Government to arrange peace,
sends for Nina and the kids.
Ten kilometres from the city, her car
is shot up by an SS zealot.

Full dress uniform. Best eye-patch.
He prepares to meet Churchill.
A voice in his head tells him
he wishes he'd failed.

*On July 20, 1944 the Führer's staff meeting was held in a temporary building.
Hitler was only slightly injured by the bomb. Stauffenberg was executed that night.
Nina von Stauffenberg died in 2006.*

II. Wilfred Owen speaks in Ripon Cathedral, September 1938

He is introduced with all ceremony
by an obsequious Dean.
He has made a friend of Bishop Bell
who persuaded him he *must speak*
now the lust for war has begun to return.

Time has treated him well.
Elected that same summer
                              to the Chair of Poetry at Oxford
beating the presumptuous young Auden.
His speech at the Union settled it.

Twenty years ago,
on his twenty-fifth birthday
he sat here all afternoon
in *Zugswang* with God.
There were periodic exchanges of fire
and long sustaining silences.

He pondered Lewis Carroll's rabbit
diving for its funk-hole
under the claws of a hawk.
He visited the shrine of feisty young Wilfred
Saint of Northumbria
                              but mainly he sat

while France receded
and the sweet green of England, at cherry-blossom time,
its unfelled trees, its unexcavated meadows,
its air, free of chlorine and cordite,
settled in his mind.

It was the day his posting changed. A tactical victory
(as he later grudgingly conceded), for God.

This is the Sunday after the Munich Agreement.
He gets up slowly, scoping the rim of the pulpit,

in a second he knows he will be trapped
in the open. All he has pursued for twenty years
against the old lie

is caught in enfilade
                    from a zigzag trench
where wickedness and weakness
form a lethal party.

He rises, raked by doubt and confusion.
He speaks of the impossibility of certainty
and yet of the urgency of the time.
He talks of meeting a ghost, now in his middle years,
and walking in dead patrol, searching for clarity.

Visiting Ripon that day
T.S. Eliot makes a note in his diary.

*Owen was killed seven days before the end of World War I. He had
published only five poems.*

III. Elizabeth at Hatfield

The tree is broad at her back. As places
for house arrest in daily danger of death go
this one has a sense of space – she has come to love it:
the way the breeze tosses unscythed grass
the way the oaks think their way through the year.

Six riders have been sent, dressed in scarlet.
She remembered afterwards thinking
scarlet might have been a good omen
a colour of celebration
for the giving of a Queen's ring.

She is reading Roger Ascham, bound in calfskin.
It is her dying sister's last cruelty
that they allow her no books but her missal
in the two days it takes
for threadbare legalities, and assembling the scaffold.

The crown passes to Spain.
The English Bible is withdrawn. Shakespeare
stays in Verona.
All books and plays are censored
in the grim halls of the Escorial.

A few terrorists persist for a while in piracy.
Their names are forgotten.

Only Pole, her kinsman, was kind
when he came to hear her last confession.
He made a good Pope, after all.

The Princess Elizabeth was sitting under a tree at Hatfield Palace on
November 17, 1558, when word was brought to her that her sister Mary's
death made her Queen.

Cardinal Reginald Pole, Mary's Archbishop of Canterbury, who had nearly
been elected Pope in 1549, died the same day.

THREE STUDIES FROM RAPHAEL

I. 'Self-Portrait'

The youth from Urbino
long hair beautiful as a girl's
who would put himself to anything:
mapping the antiquities,
redesigning the basilica,
tracing the patterns of light
across a string of cornelian
at a princess's throat.
His version of himself is someone
who somehow knows he will never be old.

II. 'Julius II'

The pope who rehearsed the wearing of those rings
through three conclaves, and twenty years
at the edge of the poisoner's stare.
Raphael cuts deep the shadows under Julius's eyes,
explores the cruel compassion of the survivor.
A young painter investigates old age -
power that has forgotten youth
and is content to commission immortality.

III. 'The Alba Madonna'

A vigorous woman, a thinker,
leans her head on a distant mountain,
looks out at a cross and beyond a cross.

The babes have zestful muscles;
they are athletes in arms, dancers in repose
against the soft haze of Umbria.

Mary as poet, as Raphael,
looks past them, past them.

III

THE APPLICATION

for T.H.

Dear Professor, I am very interested
In being part of your intriguing
Programme. I am currently taking a break from films.
I have an 'A' in everything I have ever attempted
And see little point in formal lectures
But it would be a pleasure to meet once a month
For a well-chilled manzanilla
And a discussion of Plato. The early dialogues
Are of particular interest to me.
Yours sincerely, The Blue Rose.

Dear Ms Rose, I am very glad you can fit me in
To your career break. I personally like a dry madeira
With Plato. Given your accomplishments
I recommend we engage without delay
With the dialogues on love. The College Office
Tell me your application is deficient
In respect of Programme Learning Outcomes 2-11.
However we look forward to receiving your fees.
American Express is preferred.

THE REVIEW

Frankly, I was disturbed.
                              Yes, the aggressiveness of the playing.
A very strange take on Beethoven.
                              Brilliant, yes, but lacking in balance.
Lacking most of all in taste.

Lisl is three yards from the radio, so Petr hears it,
Just in that grumpy, pensive mood she sometimes sees in him
After lovemaking. She finds the off-switch,
Lets her robe fall open as she turns.
She could after all
                              .

            But she cannot
She sees that in a second. And in the next
He is up, naked, shaking her by the shoulders.
Get out, he shouts. You disgust me, he says,

And is at the piano, still nude, obsessing
On the Appassionata, attacking the opening
Again and again, while she dresses, quietly, quietly.

She is out in the rain, Beethoven
Pounding in her head. She scrapes her car
Against a low post. She conjugates 'fuck' in every mood
In the twenty minute drive to her parents'.

She cannot let the wave hit, she tells herself. Not yet.
But when her father looks at her over his glasses,
And asks her, as he does every week, picking his moment, always,
When she's going to get a real job, she not only snaps back
That he's never encouraged her

But barrels on into how he's never loved her,
Not as her mother loved her.

Her mother does not know, any more,
The man who lives with her.
Her mother does not know, any more,
The man who is normally kind, but exercises today,
When Lisl has gone, his prerogative of cruelty,
And places her whisky three inches out of her reach.

Lisl was three yards from the radio
When the reviewers' phrases were tossed off.
Disturbing, frankly.

GETTING TO R

"Q he was sure of. Q he could demonstrate... ... he stuck at Q. He would never reach R." (Virginia Woolf, *To the Lighthouse*)

On balance, I am inclined to regard Q
As overrated. E has been a place
To meet the young, a perch from which to view
Glory, a fair finish to anyone's race.
I have sniffed at F, hinted at G.
Those at P, or even Q, are best
Company when they tramp humbly
The long moor, surprised not to be last.

Once I met a man who'd seen born
A whole alphabet. Ex-heroism.
He's now forever reporting a new unicorn,
Ziggurats that are always phantasms.
I wait, at E, for him to admit in anger
That the end of all our exploring is hunger.

THE POSTCARD

Modigliani: Female Nude, 1916

Her complexion looks Spanish
With perhaps a hint of Morocco.
The hair, pure black,
Lies on her right shoulder.
Strands escape to frame
A modest breast.

England. Early light
Across a London courtyard.
The postcard takes me other places –
Paris, and an alley in Andalusia –
A dancer in a red shift dress
Slips from the side-door of a bar.

I am all the ages
I have ever been
And inhabit many possibilities
Grasped and ungrasped,
Acting on their stages parts familiar
And those I never dared attempt.

She is long dead, and lives forever
In a painting I have long loved.
I steal away from meetings
To hide in the stern angles
Of the Courtauld
And be with her.

She leans her body
Against the red dress,
The lovely Cycladic head on one side,
The eyes closed.
She is not interested
In my adoration.

I still hanker after one flash
Of those brilliant black unseen eyes
To show she knows that a moment
Of her life, and fragments of mine,
Lie truly together
Without shame or evasion,

Even in this Protestant northern light.

MY KIND OF WOMAN

The crystallographer on the radio today.
In need of fine fibres
to hold her micro-crystals
she quite logically uses
her new baby's hair.
The child grows up loved
                          but learns to protect its head.

**

Some rangy eighteen-year-old blonde
in the final of a Grand Slam.
The opponent's return soft, dropping mid-court,
she opens her suntanned shoulders
and hits the drive volley
out of sheer uncalculated joy
                          at being alive.

**

The friend I wake up with
whose moods are the music
of the last thirty years.
Whose upturned face
whose shining eyes
ask, and give
                          peace beyond the reach of poems.

OPERATION MUSE

The body with the forged secret documents
was floated into the sea off Spain,
in the knowledge it would be passed
to the Nazis. It carried fake love-letters.
Some female spook poured out
her counterfeit heart, to build the identity
of a man who never was.
Dear Billy, it has been so long
since I have seen you. I will always remember
(blacked out by censor) on your last leave.

Poets too are fashioners of the false,
doing the police in different voices,
constructing hearts to counterfeit.
They tidy passions into pentameters,
make life a green fuse, desire a green haze.
They long to see their treacheries
smuggled across frontiers.
Once deceived, tyrants no longer trust themselves
and the shyest lovers break radio silence,
forge a joy beyond what has ever been.

HE BECAME HIS REPUTATION

Freshly retired – full of plans.
Still invited to give the odd keynote.
Delighted to shed admin,
Though he misses colleagues' banter.

He dedicates to them
The book he always meant to write
Which somehow does not
Quite say what he meant to say.

Retired and run out of projects.
Pitching up at the AGMs of charities
Hoping to be proposed for the Committee.
He would even do Treasurer.

He has a rough plan for a book
Which will be his last
But it does not seem
To get written.

Retired and just plain tired
And giving rise to a bit of concern.
Dopamine down and damn forgetful
And never expected to live like this.

His books jeer at him from his shelves.
He almost wrote one with someone who was almost
Prime Minister. Long phone-calls
To the councils of the great, long forgotten.

The notice on the short-obituaries page.
Factual. Humourless.
He inspired hundreds of the wondering young.
It does not say that.

The university library has decided that any book
Not borrowed for thirty years
Will be discarded.

The title is from Auden's poem on the death of Yeats.

ALZH--MER'S

they explain quietly beforehand
about Viola, that she no longer...
they give me an hour
to decide whether to pretend
she saves me the trouble
by telling me herself
though it takes her ten minutes
to articulate
then we track slowly across her life
driven by her need to be clear

inside me is a terror of such a diagnosis
my time with Viola
gives me new insight into my fear
I used to dread being locked in on myself
not able to explain
I retain that familiar fear
this winter day of white-grey light
grey water seen through bare trees
when loved friends are distant
deadlines ubiquitous

but know now a new twist to my anxiety
Viola shows me
as all her thoughts sail uncamouflaged
looking for harbours to land in
then are jabbed out in front of her
like the white sticks of the blind
and there is no longer the security
of keeping them hidden
at battle anchorage
no longer the luxury

of being able to pretend.

ADAM AND THE STASI

They are at work again on the Stasi files,
on roomfuls of debris, hastily reduced to shreds
as freedom closed in, as long-frustrated longing
found release, as the culture of betrayal
was betrayed, and a land of secrets
emerged, pallid and hesitant, into light.

It was disturbing, though, the light
shed on the far-off country by the first files
and their uncomfortable secrets.
For all the much-trumpeted much-novelised longing
for freedom, half a country had colluded in betrayal.
What more might be revealed by the shreds?

It is possible now to subject shreds
of the documentation of betrayal
to cage-loads of computer monkeys, bringing to light
jigsaw patterns in cheap typescript, secrets
petty and sordid, anatomies of corrupted longing.
For better or worse, the world will have the files.

Adam is quietly confident he would be in the files.
Leaned on lightly by the thought-police, some trite betrayal
inevitable, self-protection proving stronger than longing
for virtue. That much is no secret
but he fears the monkeys all the same, their reassembling into light
of what, in his history, is safely in shreds.

There are moreover happy endings in the shreds
if he assembles them to serve his own longing
to edit out past betrayal
to retell himself the best versions of secrets.
His own monkeys are constantly down among the files
working always in carefully subdued light.

He encourages others to bring to light
the inner dynamics of their longing.
That, he finds, buries his own files
deeper, conceals more neatly his own betrayal.
Besides, he knows, in his days, what pass for shreds
of happiness, soon over, safe now as secrets.

He is conscious of a longing, when he thinks of the Stasi files,
the joined-up shreds, the patterns of betrayal,
for a monkey virus, or to live in a yet more secret light.

IV

THE LOT FELL ON MATTHIAS

At the beginning of the Acts of the Apostles, Christ's disciples chose a successor
to Judas Iscariot, drawing lots between two candidates (Acts 1.21–26)

I was not at all sure I wanted it.
Judas' seat, that is.
Even as they talked it through
I could see the confusion in the group.
Choosing a twelfth seemed like superstition.

Besides, I sensed trouble ahead. I did not fear
the priests, as much as Pharisees
who would suddenly see the light
and come in knowing it all
and wanting to change everything.

I did not want it – a seat in all that contestation.
I sang the Psalms with them, broke bread,
balanced the books, kept my counsel.
In material things we held all in common –
an accountant's nightmare.

I missed most his voice.
How he laughed at me.
How he looked into my heart.
He knew, and never told anyone,
about that first day on the lakeshore.

It rained hard that day (no-one
mentions that). Raindrops bounced off the lake,
glinted as they fell. Then in the sudden
sunlight he was standing there,
robe soaked, bantering with the brothers.

I listened by a rickety shed
smelling of fish. The voice changed,
began to talk of fishing for men,
and I ducked into that stinking shed.
He saw me do it.

I would never have taken Judas' seat
but for those minutes, cowering in that shed,
before I bundled my fear into my bag
and ran up the hill towards glory.

SAUL AT THE STONING OF STEPHEN

A man was roasting nuts at a brazier.
Closer to the gate, Saul stood
With the pile of cloaks. There was one
He liked the look of, yellow stars
Woven seamless into the fabric.

He had never seen a stoning
And had thought the missiles
Would be small, hurled from a distance.
This was up close and personal,
With boulders, discarded building blocks,

The stones themselves shouting
Condemnation. There was an ugly
Blood-lust to it – he made a note
That this was to be avoided.
What had to be done

Should be done with sorrow.
He looked away at the end –
Missed the man's dying prayer.
There was an odd light – he forced himself
To focus on it – like a wound in the sky

Somewhere to the north-east.

PENTIMENTO

Change of mind is said to be a good test
of authenticity. The painterly
intelligence plays, risks – uncertainty
is alien to the copyist.

In Gethsemane we note the hesitation.
It helps us see
the genuineness, the humanness.

But for the subject himself
leaving his friends exhausted and sleeping
this was the hateful test.

Would not a consummate forger
impart pentimento to deceive?
Surely at this of all moments

he should be confident of the composition?

It was the mob, coming in from the right,
Iscariot leading,
that reassured him.

THE UNIT

New anti-terrorist measures in Britain call for a process of 'compulsory deradicalisation'.

I remember the rabbi. He was from nowhere much.
But not a man we could easily forget.
The session started well enough. He agreed
To the justice of the payment of fair taxes.

                                                    Blessed,

He said, *are the peacemakers.*
This was promising. I marked it on his chart.

His voice was extraordinary. It was just as well
There were six of us on shift
Including some of our toughest. One of us
Had even heard Richard Dawkins in the flesh.

                                                    Blessed

Are the pure in heart, the rabbi said, like sunlight
Beyond a storm, lighting up a distant sea.

This wasn't going in a good direction.
I looked around for help.

                                                    Blessed,

He insisted, *are those who hunger and thirst
After righteousness.* It was like the first kiss

                                        I ever shyly received
From the first woman I truly loved. *They shall be filled.*

We read him the sharpest chapter of *The God Delusion.*
We water-boarded him, just once or twice.
Four is the maximum quota on the Unit.

                                                    Blessed

(again, again) *are the meek.*
They shall inherit the earth. We even tried
The Church's concealment of abuse.

After that he seemed reluctant to say more
But we made him, as we do.
So quietly I could hardly hear.
                                            Blessed
Are the poor in spirit. And looking
Me straight in the eye, missing two front teeth now,
Those who know their need of God.

At Toledo, once, before the *auto-da-fé*
The prisoner was released
Without full deradicalisation.
Most of us were not minded
To repeat the mistake.

The last stanza derives from Dostoevsky's myth of Christ appearing
before the Grand Inquisitor in *The Brothers Karamazov*.

WHAT IF

What if we were only our work?
    relentless appraisal, specious promotion,
                        inexorable redundancy
    or edged-out retirement.

What if we were only our illnesses?
    A mass of scans, bilirubin levels, cytokines.
                       We exchange parameters,
    scans of masses.

What if we were only our loves?
    only the times with the ones
                       we have been naked beside
    or held, desperately, in the night?

What if in this tremendous darkness
    there were no stars
                       or they incited
    no wonder.

What if we were never as little children?

V

RETURN TO GROUND ZERO, 2012

No entry to the new memorial.
On-line booking is down
                because of the hurricane.
I lose my chance to lose my eyes
in a square pool inside a square pool
in water falling out of falling.

Instead I sit in a small church;
a choir grapples with Bach
                in a place
where firemen slept on pews,
and on boards and railings there gathered
line on line of pleas for the missing
lines about the missing.

The conductor tells the choir
                they are all over the place.
Which is what here is, eleven years on.
It will not settle into history, this jumble
of mementoes, teddy bears,
badges from fire departments across the world -
outstretched longing, letters left about longing.

Eleven years ago I looked down at Ground Zero
                still burning.
Relatives were being led in to breathe
the ruined, lachrymal air.
I am not able to drown that memory
                in neat square pools;
on-line booking is down, because of the hurricane.
There is only this jumbled hoping, this endlessly battered hoping
        about loving.

NATIONAL GALLERY CAFÉ

Mizzling rain across Trafalgar Square.
The Gallery is free. The hot water in the toilets
Is hot. Back in the high rooms the walls
Are lined with old friends – Rembrandt, Canaletto, Vermeer.
They never fail to surprise. After an hour I retreat
To a café full of compositions. The proud
Grandmother telling her sister
'He *is* a lovely little boy'. The woman in the corner,
So still while she listens, all eloquence
When she talks – she spreads her hands wide,
Sweeps long fingers across the table,
Holds her right hand to her heart, brings it
Quickly to cover her eyes.
                              I wish her friend would shut up
So I could see more of this lucid semaphore.
A stubbly youngish man, hiding under the shadow
Of a once-good raincoat, begins
The skilful nursing of a sweet milky coffee.

The grandmother meanwhile
Rails against the sheer wickedness of systems.
The Prime Minister has been re-elected. A French family
Sit down next to me. The teenage daughter –
Mohair sweater, chestnut curls - demolishes cream cake.
The little brother would rather be *anywhere*
Than here. Copies of Stubbs and van Eyck
Stare down from the wall. A student
Hoovers up granola, fixated on her Mac.
The French parents still flirt with each other
After all these years.
                              Will the new Government
Dare to charge for all this joy? Van Eyck's Giovanna,
Attending raptly to her fiancé's gestures
(while wishing with all her heart
That he had chosen a different hat)
Declines to speculate.

BEETHOVEN STRING QUARTET OP. 132; TS ELIOT, 'EAST COKER'.

From the celebration of the 50th anniversary of the interment of Eliot's ashes in St Michael's, East Coker, September 26 2015.

A state of readiness slows the air
until at last, chord by wistful chord, music
sets the molecules of the church in order,
unrushed, unclotted, striving through time
to resolution. We are released from prayer
into wonder, into longed-for space.

In a brief interval, minds dally with the space.
We watch it rearrange itself, the air
recollecting centuries given to prayer –
its rigour, its silence, its music,
the way it transmutes time.
Then the poem calls us to order.

Word by word, words in turn re-order,
craft, crystallise the space.
The poem fashions silence, attends to time,
hallows it, makes it ordinary in this blent air,
gives it pulse, slows the wandering music
in our minds, makes its contrapuntal prayer.

We are not required to invest in prayer.
We are implored to stay in these moments, in order
that our all-too-unequal music
can take leave of this space,
stream out into the Indian summer air
with less need to snatch at time.

We have been quiet here, for a time,
with bitter old Beethoven, whose prayer
for hearing will be answered only in the air
of heaven. With Mr Eliot, who in order
to make poetry, suffered and betrayed. This space
pardons him, and us. But what music

can we take away, what possible music
can hold this meaning for us? Time
sweeps it away, disperses it across space.
Not even Cranmer's Common Prayer
can clutch it back, set it in order,
but something goes with us, out into the evening air.

It is not music, for that requires time.
It is a feeling of outline, of order to air,
a space of peace and grace, beyond what prayer
can pray for.

ASSYNT FRAGMENTS

a fierce wind from the west
flicking an eagle's furled feathers.
It grips its perch, motionless.

a tall cone of rock
hiding the line of climbable ridge.
I welcome settled cloud.

the opaque sheet of rain
between two headlands, craving
enough light to show rainbows.

a deep quietness
tracing the shape of the loch shore.
A raven laughs at me,
twists away, is gone.

Assynt is a remote region of the Scottish Highlands, north of Ullapool.

THE ANIMALS OF INVERPOLLY

They rear in front of me
out of the ancient plateau.
I can tell they are animals
in disguise, because they change shape
as I steal up on them from different angles
and tune themselves to the ever-changing light
intent on being undiscovered.

Today the long one, the many-faced one
in the northwest, hides first,
darkening to a black corrugated wall.
The tallest is next, affecting
a beret of cloud, to match
the grey dust at its crest.
The littlest is the bristliest – it
has been called
an angry porcupine.

But these are not modern animals
with spats of rage and surges of joy.
They are beasts older than thought.
They have been hiding here
for nine hundred million years
fearing the rumour of tectonic coups
in the lands to the east.
Their secret is safe in my dreams
in which I stride again
up the gorge of Kirkaig
and catch the five of them

waking, stretching into the pallid dawn,
glancing about them for subduction spies,
and arguing
               as to which is the handsomest.

Inverpolly Forest contains the mountains Suilven, Canisp, Cul Mor, Cul Beag, and Stac Pollaidh. They escaped the massive thrust movements that have shaped the rest of the Scottish Highlands.

A RAINBOW – LOCH ASSYNT

Stretches flat across the loch from the foot of Quinag
to skid into the hill below the eyrie.

Contracts to a ball of light, then spreads to a disc,
now to a half-arc. Stops mid-loch, like magic
afflicted by a contractors' strike.

Now it is a straight line rainbow –
a rain-ruler.

Now a drifting elongated flying saucer,
sidling southward
into the hill.

A sheet of colour, suddenly sharpening
to a flat bow, which ends in the meadow
where the stags graze at daybreak.

Indigo and violet are at loch-level,
dyeing the water pale purple.

The high colours bend and glow, riding the surface.
Then the bow fades, and Quinag
hides in its mists.

The colours remain for a moment
as a rumour over the loch. There is thunder.

Later, where the rainbow first grew,
over to the west of the mountain,
is a curtain of rain.

It has a new beauty
born out of the colours
it has defeated.

THE TORRIDON HILLS FROM THE WEST

The horns of Alligin
like fortifications
built by a crazy king.
Liathach a line of dark-caped warriors
armed for battle.
Beinn Eighe a great silver leopard
lying on one side.
                         It is worth many jarrings of ankles and
knees
on these long steepnesses
                    to slow the eyes to see
mad castle, dark warriors, leopard sleeping.

PORTO DE CAMINO, SANTIAGO

In they stream. Only a few hundred metres more
to touch the Gate of Glory. Knee bandages
and dust-stains, from the hard track.

Young men making light of heavy packs,
determined spring in their trainers.

Young couples for whom this is some sort
of landmark, way-station, or perhaps the moment
when faiths fail to cohere.

Older couples giving thanks, or making a point,
or because one of them is dying.

Groups of teenagers, with their priest.
They sing well-chosen chants as they wait
for the crossing light to go green.

Francis of Assisi walked up this street
tired, dusty, compassionate, wolf at his heel.

Perhaps he too sang at the crosswalk. Perhaps
he waited there, arguing with his father and the Pope,
while the Archbishop's carriage passed by.

He talked with a Moor, a worker in jet.
The man had had to confess Christ to survive.

Francis forgave him his apostasy,
and blessed him, and slipped down the hill
to enter by Glory.

There was a welcoming committee of prelates
tedious with their intrigues.

Or there was no welcome, but only
a bustle of brothers with agendas
none of them brave enough to hold the wolf.

Eight hundred years on. The smoke-belching pendulum
is not swinging. Except on Fridays.

The Gate of Glory is hemmed in by scaffolding
and the sermon at the Pilgrim Mass
is obscure and protracted.

Outside, a clown is blowing giant bubbles
by the statue of horses, leaping out of water.

The bubbles wobble in the air like improvised rainbows.
Some delight in popping them,
others, footsore, still full of agendas,

are content to stand and watch
as ersatz rainbows wobble skywards.

HOLOCAUST MEMORIAL, JUDENPLATZ, VIENNA

Around the stone bunker
Walled in reversed books

Names of camps
Where Austrian Jews died.

Alphabetical. Forty-five.
No camps began with Q,
Or U, or Y.

Those are the questions
Still in our heads.

Or perhaps they are the camps
In our hearts.

CAFÉ GRIENSTEIDL, VIENNA

All cobble-clops at the carriage-stands
Behind the Hofburg's classical curves and angles.

This is a city dominated by the palaces of monarchy
Kitted out to rule Europe.

When the empire disappeared
There was a bitter, squalid, hungry time.

Power and procession returned
With swastikaed myrmidons.

Griensteidl banned
Its favourite customers.

Fingers sticky from squeezing lemon-juice
On my schnitzel.

Faint but pervasive
The smell of horse-manure.

The coppered domes of the Hofburg
Are patched with black sheeting.

There is a nice trade in memories.

LIGHT AND THE PELICAN

San Diego Harbour

Sunlight
so bright on the waters of the bay
that drops of dazzle
bounce from the surface
as though in some
alchemical rainstorm.

The pelican, beak held downwards
like a hoodlum's knife in repose
swims by the fishing platform
waiting for State handouts.
The sun catches the fine riffle of his crest-feathers,
the snake of neck.

Despairing of charity
he unfurls wings
like two great coat-hangers
and runs into the sky
for a moment clumsy, then
flowing into a long planing glide,

indwelling the air
like the light the water.
Above him
two military transports
lumber across the luminous
blue afternoon.

ISUIEN GARDEN, NARA, JAPAN

I.

A small stream passes shallowly over a fall
by the house of the tea ceremony.
Its ripples dominate the pond.

Each slow pulse plates out an upside-down maple tree,
mutes and pales the peach of its leaves.
It is the first turn to autumn.

A single bloom shows on the water-lilies –
sharp cream against their puckered green mat.
A very old pine juts out on stilts.

The pond is rimmed with close-fitting boulders.
They and their reflections make a double wall,
an undefence of this timelessness.

A quantum of breeze catches the island, catches and dies.
The bridge is a single block of worn slate.
I leave muddy footprints.

II.

I clump my body down in the teahouse
to watch the moss grow
and listen to the crickets sing.
Even the gardener's sweatshirt
smells of incense.

The loveliness of this place
is completely impassive.
I feel I could add to it only by letting these pages
dissolve in one of the ponds.

I have written in the bronze-red of that water-lily.
I have green in my pen to match the viridian maples.
My inks would sidle slowly into the water
momentarily making new curves
between the ancient boulders.

I could stay in Isuien
and dissolve poems
or go home and place a stone
more exactly
in my own garden.